Shattering Glass Ceilings:

NO OBSTACLE TOO GREAT FOR GOD'S ENABLING POWER

Christine Low

authorHOUSE®

AuthorHouse™ UK
1663 Liberty Drive
Bloomington, IN 47403 USA
www.authorhouse.co.uk
Phone: UK TFN: 0800 0148641 (Toll Free inside the UK)
          UK Local: (02) 0369 56322 (+44 20 3695
          6322 from outside the UK)

Published by AuthorHouse   03/18/2022

ISBN: 978-1-6655-9696-1 (sc)
ISBN: 978-1-6655-9697-8 (e)

Print information available on the last page.

Any people depicted in stock imagery provided by Getty Images are models,
and such images are being used for illustrative purposes only.
Certain stock imagery © Getty Images.

COVER ILLUSTRATION BY BEV STEAD

This book is printed on acid-free paper.

Scripture quotations are taken from the Holy Bible,
New International Version®, NIV®.
Copyright © 1973, 1978, 1984 by Biblica, Inc.™
Used by permission of Zondervan. All rights reserved worldwide.

To my husband and soulmate, John,
without whose unswerving support,
encouragement and faith in me,
this book would never have come into being

and to all those who experience the
restrictions of a 'glass ceiling'.

Contents

Foreword

One of the earliest Christian maxims I was told in the 1960s was a line from a hymn by Charles Wesley: 'Faith ... laughs at impossibilities and cries, "It shall be done!"'

Chris Low's book, *Shattering Glass Ceilings*, is a wonderful embodiment of this statement. She shares some of the fundamental battles she has faced in her life, ranging from her abandonment by her father when she was a young child, the destructive and alarming effects of multiple sclerosis as a wife and mother, and the gender prejudices within the Church of England as she pursued her calling to be an ordained priest. Chris might not have been laughing all the time, but she continued to believe in herself and her calling and so committed herself to the focus that nothing was going to stop her moving forward in her life.

The adventures of her faith and journey are told in a very engaging and helpful style. You are drawn into her story and find yourself examining your own story. One of the major themes to emerge as she shares her many experiences of the Christian healing ministry is that God wishes to engage us all in his care of persons and care of worlds. The weaknesses and limitations we perceive in ourselves actually qualify us for this calling by God.

A second major theme is that we must resist the pressure

to let other people determine what we can be or do in life. Chris encourages us all to live an open-horizon life where only God sets the boundaries within which we are to flourish as the people we are called to be. It is an inspirational story that Chris shares, but she would not want our appreciation to end there. Her book is a wake-up call to laugh at the impossible prejudices and failures which would stop our capacity for living to the full dimensions of our personhood, and gives us the empowerment to cry 'It shall be done!'

THE REVEREND DR RUSS PARKER
Author of *Healing Wounded History*

Preface

I have spoken on many occasions about the testimony of my healing from multiple sclerosis and frequently been asked to put it in writing. Without the inheritance left me by my mother, this would still be a few jottings and a future hope. (Thanks, Mum.)

As I began to put it together, the book evolved from a testimony to an inspirational guide for stepping out in faith and trusting to God's enabling in order to fulfil one's God-given potential. I hope readers will find in these pages the encouragement to face down detractors and to refuse to be held back by the limitations imposed upon them by their background, gender, or any other restricting circumstances.

I suppose this will not surprise those who know me. I was a teacher for thirty years prior to ordination and always sought to encourage my pupils to have faith in themselves and not to be held back by the opinions or prejudices of others. In addition, my years as a Soroptimist have involved me in campaigning and practical actions to support women and girls locally, nationally, and internationally so that they reach their potential.

As a result of the healing I received, the Christian healing ministry has been at the heart of my ministry both before and since ordination. It should come as no surprise then that the healing ministry is a thread woven into this book.

I wanted *Shattering Glass Ceilings* to be inspirational and Bible-based, so you will find each chapter begins with a relevant verse from scripture and that other scriptures are included throughout. God's Word is the greatest inspiration of all, and in it the reader may find hope and encouragement as well as clear direction for their lives.

I am grateful to the Reverend Jane Emson for allowing me to share her story and to Sister Sandra Nicholls for her contribution. Also to the staff at AuthorHouse for all their help and guidance.

Introduction

Have you ever been told that you cannot fulfil a dream, had your aspirations crushed, or simply felt that you were unworthy? Do these experiences have their root in prejudice on the part of your detractors, society's attitudes and rules, or your own low self-worth? If your answer to any of the above is yes, then this book is for you.

Looking back over my lifetime, I am grateful to have lived through a period of huge change in societal attitudes and long-held prejudices, particularly in relation to women. I remember my grandmother speaking about experiencing the emancipation of women and the part she played, along with so many other ordinary women, in supporting it.

I have experienced first-hand the frustrations and restrictions of gender-shaped glass ceilings in my own life and times, and I have celebrated with my sisters as those ceilings came crashing down one by one. I have fought prejudice in all its evil faces at every opportunity and given thanks as the restrictions it imposes have gradually been eroded. Yet we still have far to go before our world truly embraces the apostle Paul's words to the Galatians: 'There is neither Jew nor Greek, slave nor free, male nor female, for you are all one in Christ' (Gal. 3:28).

By God's grace, I was healed of multiple sclerosis and

enabled to follow his call to ordination. The road was far from easy, as all pioneers can tell you, but through God's Holy Spirit and the support of many good people, it became possible. Along the way I learned many lessons, not least being to trust to God's empowering and to refuse to allow the prejudices of others to determine who I am and what I can become. I hope that this book will encourage others to step out in faith into whatever direction God calls them.

Serving in the healing ministry for over forty years, I have seen God's hand at work on multiple occasions and in many circumstances and know from first- hand experience that trusting in his grace and the guidance of his Holy Spirit enables ordinary men and women to do great things in his name. May you, my readers, be encouraged to listen to his promptings and take that first step in order to play your part in bringing in his kingdom here on earth.

.

1

A Child of God

> How great is the love the father has
> lavished on us, that we should be called
> children of God! (1 Peter 3:1 NIV)

SHUDDERS RACKED THE CHILD'S BODY AS THE ICY COLD
bit through her dressing gown. As she perched on the
stairs in the dark, it was hard to tell how much of the
shivering was caused by the temperature and how
much by the deep, gnawing fear that had become such
a part of her.

The moonlight gleamed palely through the landing
window, which was rimed with Jack Frost's tracings.
Breath fogged in the chilly air and was held. Every fibre
strained to hear the slightest sound—anything to indicate
that the others were still there in the room below. Not
a sound. The child struggled to decide whether it was
worth the reprimands that would follow to go down
and open the door on some pretext or other. No, better
to edge nearer the door, trying with each cautious step
to avoid the creaking treads, so familiar now from long
practice.

Desperation for reassurance that they were indeed still there overcame fear. A cautious step down onto the next stair, a pause to listen, then another step. Was that a sound from underneath?

Suddenly, in a heartbeat, the surrounding air changed from ice cold to an all-pervading warmth. And with it a voice—gentle, loving, and achingly familiar—yet somehow unknown.

'Don't be afraid, my little one. All is well. You will not be abandoned. You are truly loved, both by them and by me. Go to bed and sleep. You will not be forsaken, and I will always be with you.'

Filled with peace and the comfort of that promise, the child returned to bed and slept. Never again was she to wake terrified that she had been abandoned.

That child was me. Even now, over sixty-five years later, that memory is as fresh and powerful as it was then. In those days, God was still portrayed as more of an authoritarian figure than as the 'Abba' to whom Jesus referred. The revelation of his love and care has formed me, and filled me with a deep desire to help others to know the depth of God's love for them.

When I was four years old, my father left my mother, me, and my two younger brothers and returned to his family home on the other side of the village where I grew up. A few months later, he collected me from my mother and took me to live with him, his mother, and two sisters. To my five-year-old self, it felt as though my mother had now rejected me.

Less than a year later, my father left for work one day and didn't return. I still remember that day, for he left the house without kissing me goodbye. An unreasoning fear consumed me as I ran after him down the steps, calling to him. Was it a premonition? When he didn't return, there was great consternation, whispered conversations, and no answers to my questions. 'Where's my daddy? Why hasn't he come home? When will he be back?'

It took my grandmother eighteen months and the services of a private detective to find him—though long before then, it must have been clear what had happened. It isn't easy to keep secrets in a small village. He had simply walked away from us all in order to be with another man's wife. Apparently, she was the cause of his original defection. They had gone to London and remained there for the rest of my father's life. It was nearly three years before I saw him again.

So by the time God gave me that wonderful assurance, I had a deep-seated fear and expectation of abandonment by those I loved and trusted. When first taken from my mother, I had been told—and this continued to be the case as I grew—that my father had been informed that she was ill-treating and neglecting me. To this was later added the information that my mother hadn't the finances to look after both me and my two brothers.

(Small wonder, since my father frequently defaulted on the maintenance payments awarded by the court!) So in my mind it was clear that I was not as important as my brothers.

These half-truths and lies, along with many others, meant that I grew up to despise and reject my mother. Many years passed before that rift was healed and our relationship restored. It says much for my mother's love and patience that she welcomed me so wholeheartedly when I finally recognised the truth and sought to make amends.

In the months following my father's departure, the constant, nagging fear of being abandoned by those I loved and trusted led me time and again to leave my bed to listen for any sounds from the living room below in order to reassure myself that my remaining family was still there. Strange how such deeply damaging events can remain so clear in our memories long after their effects have been healed.

In those pre-TV days, when more often than not my grandmother and aunts would be reading, there were few sounds to reassure me. Leaving my bed and disturbing them with whatever excuse I could manufacture always got me into trouble. Yet the fear of being abandoned frequently outweighed the fear of retribution.

After that encounter with God, our loving Heavenly Father became very real to me and was, in truth, the father I longed for. God became the presence who loved and cared for me and who, unlike my biological father, would never abandon me, becoming the one on whom I could safely rely. It was to be many years before I felt able to fully trust and rely upon another human being— that person being John, my husband of fifty-one years.

Despite the years of theological study that taught my mind to comprehend that God is neither male nor female and should not be limited by our understanding of gender, and despite all that I do and have done in bringing about justice and equality for women and girls in very many areas of life, in my heart God is still and always will be Abba, Daddy.

I took all my troubles, woes, and hopes to him, knowing he would listen. Sometimes, however, answered prayer had a sting in the tail. As my eleventh birthday approached, so did the eleven-plus, the exam that determined who would attend grammar school. I was able enough but poor at focusing on my work. My mind was often a jumble of confused thoughts and anxieties. A teacher's nightmare, I squandered my abilities and underachieved in almost all areas except reading.

I had ambition, though: I wanted to pass the eleven-plus and go to grammar school. My grandmother had always stressed the importance of obtaining the best education possible. She wanted me to be independent and able to live my life without relying on a man to provide for me. As I grew up, this became a central ambition for me.

I was determined never to be left in the difficulties in which my mother had found herself.

But there was another, less edifying reason for my ambition. I had overheard my father comment rather disparagingly that I wasn't grammar school material, and I'd be sure to fail the exam. How I wanted to prove him wrong. Maybe if I did, he'd love me and spend more time with me. Forlorn hope!

I prayed, pleading with God to help me to pass the exam and promising heaven knows what if he answered my pleas. I tried to focus more on my studies and prepare for the exam. My stomach was in a permanent knot of anxiety as the exam day approached. On that fateful, and for many life-changing, day we found ourselves sitting in the classroom, desks spaced to make it difficult to cheat. In an absolute silence broken only by a muffled sob from one for whom it was just all too much, we sweated over the papers before us. The time passed in a blur as I desperately tried to answer the questions in front of me to the very best of my ability.

The joy of receiving the news that I had passed was somewhat overshadowed by the discovery that I, one of the less promising pupils, had achieved the highest marks. How could this be? The head clearly suspected mischief and checked to see who my nearest neighbours had been. Fortunately for me, all those near me had failed the exam quite comprehensively. Otherwise, I would have been denounced as a cheat, which I most certainly was not. It did make me wonder, though, about whether I should be a little more careful in what I asked God for!

Living in a small village in the 1950s, I struggled with the sense of being looked down on for being the child of divorced parents and for the disgrace of my father's adultery and disappearance. Add to that my mother's nationality: she was German, and you can imagine there was already plenty of gossip. With the Second World War still a very clear memory, there was bound to be prejudice against someone of German nationality. Strange, isn't it, the way people can judge a child by the origins or actions of their parents.

Yet there were many who were kind and who encouraged me in many ways. To them I am deeply grateful. Our lovely neighbours, 'Aunty' Clare and 'Uncle' Fred, were always a haven of love and acceptance, angels put there by God. It was Clare who, following the unwelcome discoveries I made after my father's sudden death, gave me the space to vent my anguish, distress, and insecurity.

I had been given to understand that my father and Marjorie had married following his divorce from my mother, but such was not the case. This was one of several revelations in the aftermath of his death which left me questioning the truth of much that I had been told. Aunty Clare gently helped me to understand that my mother was not the monster she had been portrayed to be and encouraged me to reach out to Mum. It couldn't have been easy for her; deeply loyal, she knew that my grandmother and Aunt Daphne would see this as a betrayal on her part if I ever shared our conversation with them. Their friendship ran deep, and they had been close for many years.

Within our parish church, whatever was said or thought privately, I always found kindness, acceptance, and encouragement. The church was the epicentre of my little world. There my faith blossomed, first through Sunday school, and then in my teenage years through the youth club and Sunday evening study groups at the vicarage, alongside the regular rhythm of Sunday worship.

I owe so much to my adored Aunt Edna, or 'Eddie' as our son later christened her. She was my father's eldest sister and was working in London when I was first taken away from my mother. A few years later, she returned to the family home and a job in the nearby town. Like so many of her generation, Eddie had lost her fiancé to the war and never married. She was one of the many unmarried women who formed the backbone of our churches and communities. One of her many acts of service was to pioneer the setting up of a youth club in our church hall for the young people of our area. In the absence of anyone else willing to take on the responsibility of being the youth leader, she undertook the necessary training and found others to help her run the club.

It was Eddie who nurtured my faith and encouraged

me to attend church with her. We would talk about all manner of things, and she always encouraged me to explore and think things through. Eddie was my advocate who could be relied upon to talk the others around into letting me join my friends for various activities as I grew older. Without her, life would have been very frustrating and often lonely. It was also Eddie who introduced me to the joys of amateur theatre, something that brought me a huge amount of joy and increased confidence over the years.

Through Eddie, I came to know a lovely couple, Joyce and Graham Johnson, who became a constant in my life, opening windows onto the wider world, encouraging me to use what talents I had and to reach for a career. Through them, I glimpsed what it was for a couple to be truly united in love and perceived a template for a happy family life.

I don't think that any of these lovely people ever realised just what a blessing they were. So often, God draws such people into our lives for a time of need. They are life's encouragers, waymarkers, and bringers of hope. Often unaware of their impact and the legacy they leave, the world is blessed by their presence. We often fail to realise the impact that we can have on the lives of those around us simply by taking the time to listen, encourage, and affirm them.

My life growing up in a small Cornish village in the 1950s was very different from that experienced by my children twenty years later and by my grandchildren today. So much has changed, much for the better, particularly for girls. In those days 'a woman's place' was still regarded as 'in the home'. Pupils still left school at fourteen, although that was soon raised to fifteen, and many parents failed to encourage their daughters to aspire to higher education.

I remember the first time that I encountered the concept of inequality for the female gender. I was about nine years old, and coming from a seafaring family, I loved the sea. My paternal grandfather had been a master mariner. Paintings of his ship, the *St Austell*, hung on our living room walls. My dream was to join the navy and go to sea. Imagine my disgust when I was told in no uncertain terms that the only way that I could join the navy was as a nurse or in some sort of shore-based clerical post. No chance of actually going to sea for a mere girl! What a delight it was recently to witness my great niece go through officer training at the Royal Naval College.

Later, in my teens, I was even more horrified to discover that one of my earliest friends was not allowed to stay on at school to study for her A levels, despite being very bright. Her father decreed that it would be a waste of time and money as she would only get married and have babies. Instead of going on to higher education, she left school to take up a job in an office. Little wonder then that throughout my life I have championed the cause of equality for women and girls and sought to break through those glass ceilings that held us down and prevented us from reaching our potential.

It has been a great joy and privilege to be a member of Soroptimist International, a women's service organisation dedicated to improving the lives of women and girls locally, nationally, and internationally and to work on their many projects. They have a seat for women's affairs on the United Nations because of their work through 'Programme Action' projects and really do 'make a difference'.

Looking back, I realise how fortunate I was to have around me strong women who encouraged me to study and make the very best of my life. With their encouragement, at the age of eighteen I left Cornwall and went to teacher training college in London. There I encountered other strong women who had forged their careers and made a real difference in the world.

Even in education, however, there were still many signs of discrimination and injustice against women; but more of those later...

2

God's Provision

God will meet all your needs according
to his glorious riches in Christ Jesus.
(Philippians 4:19 NIV)

DESPITE THEIR LIMITED MEANS, MY GRANDMOTHER AND
aunts ensured that I went on to higher education, made
possible also thanks to the government's grant system,
which covered all the fees and gave me a termly grant
for living expenses, books, and the train fare to and
from college each term. Along with holiday jobs, this
support ensured that I stayed solvent. After three years
at teacher training college in London, I qualified as a
teacher and began my first job—and discrimination
once more raised its ugly head.

One ridiculous incident I well remember occurred during
my first year as a teacher. I was teaching six- to seven-
year-olds, and it was a bitterly cold winter in the late
sixties, the days of the miniskirt. We were an all-female
staff, and we asked the headmistress whether we might
be permitted to wear trousers to school, stressing that
they would be smart—trouser suits, even. Whilst she
supported our request, our head had to clear it first with

the education authority. Back came an unequivocal no. It would be most unsuitable for women to wear trousers to school and was not to be countenanced. Hmm, so it was OK to be constantly bending down to little six-year-olds in our miniskirts, but quite unthinkable that we should wear anything as practical and modest as a pair of trousers! Imagine the reaction to such a rule today, or even the perceived necessity of making such a request in the first place.

Shortly after qualifying as a teacher, I married John. Here was another answer to prayer, for I had asked God to bless me with a husband who would truly love and understand me and on whom I could rely completely. The early years of married life were hard, with very little money and no family nearby to offer support, but we survived. John had returned to college to train as a teacher, and with his grant and my salary, we managed—just.

Then shortly after we were married, I became pregnant. Our five-year plan had suddenly conflated to less than a year! A kindly intentioned friend told us we could obtain a grant from the students' union to cover the cost of a termination at a private clinic. Such a step was unthinkable: this was our baby, created through our love and infinitely precious. We'd cope ... somehow. Often during the following tough two years, we were aware of God's hand on us, helping us through. Three occasions among many stand out in my memory.

The first occurred just after our first wedding anniversary, when Pierren, our son, was just two months old. His first Christmas was so hard. By then, I had given up my job in order to be a full-time mum to Pierren. I couldn't bear to put my tiny baby into a nursery while I returned to work, and I had managed to get a job teaching English as a foreign language two evenings a week, when John was at home to care for Pierren, but as the job didn't start until January, life was a hand-to-mouth affair. Then disaster struck: we were burgled, and the contents of our electricity meter were stolen. The bill was due any day, so the burglar did very well out of it, but we were left with a bill we couldn't pay. We prayed, and a couple of days later the post brought a Christmas gift from my aunt Ruth. She had sent us money for Christmas, so at least the bill was paid. We were so grateful.

The second answer to prayer came a few days later, on Christmas Eve, in true Santa Claus tradition. Christmas dinner was going to be a sad affair of sausage and mash, until in the late afternoon of Christmas Eve there was a knock on the door. Our friend Roger, a butcher whose parents were hoteliers, was standing there holding a large chicken ready prepared for the oven.

'Here you go,' he said. 'This is my Christmas bonus. I'm hoping you can take it off my hands. I'm off to catch the train home, and no way am I carrying this all the way to Torbay. Talk about coals to Newcastle!' That chicken lasted several days, again a cause for rejoicing and thanksgiving. Isn't it wonderful the way that God uses us, his people, to bring his blessings to those in need?

My third and very significant example of an answer to prayer occurred a few years later. We were in North Devon, and John had begun his teaching career at a boarding school for boys aged eleven to sixteen, who in those days were classified as 'emotionally and behaviourally disturbed'. I taught there for a few hours each week while Pierren played happily on a farm in the care of friends.

We lived in a schoolhouse for the first year but then managed to obtain a mortgage for a modest three-bedroomed terraced house in South Molton. With plans to have a second child, we had been very careful to keep well within our budget when choosing our new home. This was to prove to be a huge blessing. January 1973 saw us move in, and I was sure that I was pregnant, though it was early days. However, a dark cloud swiftly loomed on the horizon, as the repayments on the mortgage increased month after month, beginning even before we were settled into our new home. At first, we were not too concerned, as we'd budgeted carefully and could afford the extra cost.

Unfortunately for us, this was the beginning of a terrible time for homeowners as mortgage rates climbed and climbed to a whopping 15 per cent. We were desperate, tears and prayers as we faced an uncertain future: there was no way out, we'd have to sell our home. But God was good. We managed to find a buyer and moved out in August, just a month before our second child, Sonja, was due. Unlike many others who found themselves in a similar situation, we managed to escape falling into negative equity, but we hadn't a penny left in our savings.

I must confess that during this terrible experience John's faith was much stronger than mine. He was utterly convinced that God would see us through the crisis. I, on the other hand, lay awake at night, feeling our second child moving in my womb and wondering what would become of us all if we found nowhere to live. Finding somewhere to rent for a young family in rural North Devon was far from easy. Cottages were either tied accommodation for farm labourers (and farmers didn't want to risk letting them as such to a young family they might struggle to move out, should they need to employ farmworkers and provide them with accommodation) or they were holiday lets, much more lucrative and far less trouble than long lets. I even spoke to the local council official about possible council housing and was told they didn't expect to provide housing for the likes of teachers!

John's headmaster, who with his wife also owned the school, came to the rescue, offering one of the empty staff cottages as a temporary measure. But it was going to be needed for a new house parent in a few short months' time so could only be a stopgap. As our search for a permanent home continued to prove fruitless, a colleague of John's stepped in and persuaded a local farming family to let us rent their empty farmworker's cottage. John's headmaster clinched the deal for us by guaranteeing to organise accommodation should the cottage be needed for a farmworker. We had a roof over our heads, but still no real long-term security.

Interest rates gradually returned to a more acceptable level, and there was news of new houses being built on the edge of the nearby town. Prices were kept down to help local families. John did the maths (well, he was a maths teacher!) and we could afford it. But how on earth would we get the deposit together? All our meagre savings had gone on paying the inflated mortgage for our previous house.

More prayers, and again God was faithful. A good friend from our London days heard of our struggles and offered the full amount of the deposit. She had come into a large sum of money and was determined to help. Initially, she insisted it be a gift, but we persuaded her to allow us to repay the loan as and when we could. We were so very grateful. Just before our daughter's second birthday, we moved into our new home. Central heating, double glazing, and cavity wall insulation—it felt like the lap of luxury!

However, remembering what had happened with our first house, I was desperate to ensure that we would never be in that position again. I started job hunting. Again, prayers were answered, and I managed to get a full-time job teaching in the pre-prep department of a small private school some ten miles away. There was a nursery class which Sonja could join the following term, so both children would travel to and from school with me. The concessionary rate offered to staff made it just about doable, and there were no worries about after-school cover as I journeyed back from work. Friends who had looked after both children previously while I did some part time teaching continued to provide care for Sonja during the summer term, and she joined Pierren and me in September.

I had never intended returning to full-time work so early in the children's lives but felt there was no option, so my teaching career took off once more. The years flew by, and I switched to teaching English at the nearby comprehensive school, where I became first head of the special needs department and then head of year, remaining there for twenty-two years. It was here that I once again encountered the evils of the 'glass ceiling' for women. About a year after joining the school, I was promoted to Grade 2. This incensed an older male colleague, who wrote a letter of complaint to the head and governors and, when this elicited a less than satisfactory response, another to his union. Apparently, to his mind, it was unthinkable that a young woman (I was thirty-three at the time) should be promoted so quickly to the same grade as himself. What was the world coming to?

I remember the words of another colleague at the time, a woman of strong mind and determination, indeed a force majeure. She was a head of year herself and told me that within that school all women experienced a glass ceiling beyond which they could not rise. No woman could attain the heights of senior management nor head up a key department (English, maths, or science). Basically, being head of year was the highest one could go, not that it stopped her and others from trying.

Things did improve, however. A few years later under a new headmaster, we had our first women on the senior management team, both having been promoted from within the school. Soon, both the maths and English departments were headed by women, followed a few years later by the science department. Later still, the same headmaster was succeeded by a woman.

Throughout my career I was determined to encourage girls to make the very best of their abilities and to aim high, never allowing their gender or any other perceived difficulties to hold them back. I delighted to see them push back the barriers and take their rightful place in life, little expecting that my own turn at major 'ceiling bashing' was just around the corner.

I was healthy as a whole but began to find myself suffering from dizzy spells and a lack of energy. Occasionally, my coordination was a bit off too, but nothing to ring alarm bells—or so I thought. However, my doctor was concerned enough to send me for a brain scan, and the results were devastating. I was diagnosed as having multiple sclerosis (MS). Amazingly, when I went to see him to receive the results of the scan, he didn't tell me it was MS; he said it was nothing to worry about, just one of those things with the inner ear, and he'd give me some pills to sort out the dizzy spells. I'd had occasional problems with my ears over the years, since an operation at the age of two, and so thought no more of it.

The bouts of tiredness I put down to my busy life, with the demands of my job and being a mum, chasing from fencing classes with our son to gymnastics with our daughter, Cubs and Brownies, and all the usual activities. Then there was our involvement with the church and the discovery of the healing ministry. Friends often said that they felt tired just thinking of all that I did! For his part, John was teaching at a boarding school and had evening and weekend duties on top of his teaching, so most of the after-school activities fell to me.

Five years later we moved to a nearby town, and not long after settling into our new home I caught the flu. However, the symptoms shifted, and I found I couldn't get out of bed without falling over. Utter exhaustion smothered me; I had never felt so ill in all my life. John sent for the doctor. At the end of the consultation, the doctor shifted uncomfortably in his chair then delivered the blow. Very gently, he explained that for some reason best known to himself, my former doctor had not told me that the brain scan showed that I had MS. It was a disease he himself had little knowledge of, so he promised to find out all he could. He made an appointment for me to see him to plan how to deal with this devastating intrusion in my life.

Eager to help, my dear friend, Claire, gave me a book to read, an autobiographical account by a journalist of her life as a young mother with MS. She had done a lot of research and found The Naomi Bransom Trust, a charity then based at Wessex University which researched MS and its effects. Professor Field, who ran the research, had come up with several positive ways of managing the disease which the author had found invaluable. With my GP's support, I made an appointment to see Professor Field. His advice and support were life-changing.

Multiple sclerosis is a disease of the central nervous system so can affect any part of the body at any time and is very unpredictable. Basically, the body's immune system attacks the central nervous system, creating plaques which block the 'messages' travelling to and from the brain. It's a bit like the 'crossed wires' we used to get on the old landline telephone system. Its effects vary from person to person, as does their severity. I was very fortunate in that mine was of the slow-moving variety. Exacerbations were often triggered by infections—indeed, anything affecting the immune system could cause an exacerbation. When in remission, I could function normally to the eye of the casual observer; at least this was so in the early days.

Have you ever been aboard a ship on a rough sea? If so, you will know how it feels to be staggering about with little control of your movements and with your coordination rather unreliable. That is a sensation from which I suffered very frequently for many years, though on terra firma and not at sea. I hasten to add that it did not result from an overindulgence in alcohol, either! From occasional bouts of dizziness, exhaustion, and lack of coordination, the disease progressed to have more far-reaching effects. Mostly, on a daily basis, I suffered from lack of coordination, dizzy spells of varying intensity, occasional slurring and muddling of speech, and cramps and spasms. Underlying these and never far away was the dragging exhaustion known to all MS sufferers. I used to describe its effects as 'trying to swim through treacle'.

I loved taking our dog, Heinz, for walks. Our bungalow was a short walk from the riverside Tarka Trail, accessed through steeply descending woodland. One warm, sunny day, Heinz and I set off down the path and out along the trail. It was a beautiful walk, and we revelled in the freedom of the light breeze which carried with it the scent of the sea as we wandered along beside the estuary. But by the time that we reached the woodland on our return journey, the old enemy was beginning to make its presence felt. My steps slowed, and my feet dragged, stumbling a little as I struggled to lift them. I felt as though I were wearing lead boots.

As we began our ascent, I looked up at the steeply climbing track I'd have to negotiate and breathed a prayer for strength to make it to the top. As I rested against a tree trunk, the prospect of actually reaching the top seemed impossible. Forcing one step in front of the other, I began the excruciatingly slow climb. I didn't know whether to pray for someone to appear and give me a much-needed hand to reach the top or simply to beg for a boost of energy and strength to get myself home. The first would be a sore dent to my independent streak and, dare I admit it, my pride; but my situation just then seemed so lonely and hopeless that a human presence would have been very welcome.

How different the situation would be today, with a mobile phone in one's pocket ready to call on the family's assistance in a moment. Unfortunately for me, that possibility was still a few years off. I struggled on, making painfully slow progress, until I reached the steepest part. My will could drive my unwilling legs no further, and I sank to the ground.

Heinz looked at me enquiringly, and I was tempted to send him home, knowing that his appearance without me would bring someone looking for me, as our daughter was sure to be home by now. The thought of the consternation and worry his lone appearance would cause made me reconsider; besides, persuading him to leave my side would probably prove impossible. He had always been my shadow, and when, as now, I was struggling with the MS, he wouldn't leave my side. With a huge effort I struggled to my knees, offering up another heartfelt prayer for divine assistance. The appearance of a big, strong guardian angel would be most welcome at this moment!

Well, if I couldn't walk this last steep part of the path, then I'd darned well crawl it. I pushed aside the thought of embarrassment if someone saw me in this state, struggling on like a toddler learning to crawl. After what seemed like hours, and with frequent stops, I reached the top and rested one last time. With a final supreme effort, I pushed myself to my feet and tottered the last few yards to our front door. That was the last time I walked any distance alone. In response to my family's pleas, I limited my solo walks to the short circuit along the top path of the woodland that ran along the back of neighbouring houses, where help would be at hand. Oh, the indignity of it!

There were many losses as the disease bit. Greatest among them was having to cease acting. The amateur theatre had been a source of great joy and fulfilment over the years, and at one point I was taking part in an average of three productions a year. With the increasing unpredictability and effects of MS, I could not risk accepting roles only to withdraw at the last minute and let everyone down. Also, I needed to conserve all my energy to do my job. Much as I loved acting, I was not prepared to let my pupils or colleagues down, and remaining on top of my game was essential if I were to continue to teach.

Over time, I learned various coping and masking strategies. For example, I found it best to place my cup on the back of my hand and slide it from there onto the tabletop, thus avoiding smashing it into the table or letting go too soon and dropping it. Holding onto the cup until all the liquid had been drained was another safe strategy. My time coaching gymnasts helped me to control my balance and avoid the 'rolling drunk' gait I dreaded to exhibit when anywhere public. I used to spot gymnast-style as I walked, locating a point at eye level to focus on, and on bad days I would traverse the school corridors with one hand running along the wall.

My colleagues and pupils were very supportive throughout this tough time. I was so blessed to be in such a lovely school and could not have continued with my beloved teaching without the support of my head and colleagues. Seeing me struggling on bad days, one good friend would tell me at lunchtime to go and have a rest and she'd deal with any issues needing my attention. I was also given indoor break-time duties because my body's 'thermostat' ceased to function properly, meaning I could go from feeling slightly chilly to hypothermic in no time. Pupils were always ready to carry books and help in myriad small ways which made life easier and helped me to function with a good degree of normality for much of the time.

John was my rock throughout this dark and difficult time. Sometimes I was so exhausted at the end of a teaching day that I would go home and collapse into bed. John would get the meal and do whatever needed to be done and wake me after a couple of hours so that I could eat and prepare for the next day. He developed hairdressing skills, learning to put rollers in my hair, and even became adept at putting on my tights for me. He supported me in every imaginable way. I struggled with the inevitable loss of independence and learned, unwillingly, to be the one to receive help instead of offering it—and to do so with grace.

Gradually the effects of the disease became more marked and impinged more and more on my life and functions. Fortunately, by then the children were in their late teens, independent but still a huge support when at home. Pierren was working in a bank some miles away, and Sonja was at chiropractic college. There was increased well-meaning pressure from my doctor to apply for early retirement on the grounds of ill health. Teaching was considered to be one of the worst possible careers for anyone with an autoimmune disease like MS. There was too much exposure to all manner of infections, in addition increased pressures and stress.

We had moved to a bungalow so that as my mobility decreased I would not have to manage stairs. I knew I was facing a time when I would have to use a wheelchair to get around. Surprisingly, for one so active, I was able to face this with a degree of equanimity. I even managed to convince myself that I could continue to teach from a wheelchair. Over a period of time, the strength in my arms waned. I could no longer reach up to write on a blackboard so was obliged to use an overhead projector instead. No computer linked white screens in those days!

On one occasion, a year before I was healed, my eyes lost their ability to focus properly, so that I was effectively blind. This devastating situation lasted for eight weeks, with no one able to tell me whether the situation would return to normal, remain as it was, or worsen. That was the most terrifying experience I've ever had. Again, prayer and the support of family and friends got me through.

One of the hardest things to live with was the uncertainty that such a disease brings. No one could tell me how the disease would progress, and I never knew from day to day how it would affect me in either the short or long term. Symptoms, such as the near blindness, might go away again, remain, or become worse. I was so grateful for the support of my family, friends, and colleagues.

The letter of James in the New Testament (James 5:13–16) reminds us that when we are sick, we should call the elders of the church to pray for us and anoint us in the name of the Lord. He tells us that the prayer offered in faith will make the sick person well. In my need I turned to my church family for this help. The prayer of Christian friends and family, together with receiving the laying on of hands and my own faith in God's love and mercy, kept me going through some very dark and uncertain times. I was fortunate in that I never felt that I had to face this awful disease alone. Besides my family and friends, I also had the comfort and support of our Lord's presence and love.

Mother Julian of Norwich wrote these words:

> As long as Christ could suffer—he did suffer, and he sorrowed for us. And now that he is risen and can suffer no more— he suffers with us.

Again and again I would find myself struggling to stay on my feet, and to get through a working day. I received healing time and again through the laying on of hands, anointing, and prayer. Although over all those years I was not cured of the disease as I longed to be, I know beyond any shadow of doubt that our Lord did heal me, that each time healing was asked for it was received—though often, at the time, in unrecognised ways.

I am certain that whenever we pray to our loving God for healing, whether for ourselves or another, that prayer is answered. It isn't always noticeable physically, but there is healing. Our Lord knows what we need most and recognises something that we often forget: we are body, mind, and spirit. He deals with what most needs to be healed. Our physical bodies, so important to us, are in fact the least important of all.

I know that over those years he healed me in many ways which opened the door for the final healing of the disease. He healed me of sin, of bad habits, of hang-ups, of resentments and past hurts, and of my failure to forgive my father. He taught me in my darkest times how completely I could rely on him and how much he loved me. Finally, in his time and in accordance with his purpose, when I finally accepted his call to the ordained ministry and bent my will in obedience to his, he healed me completely of multiple sclerosis.

3

Healed to Serve

The prayer offered in faith will make
the sick person well. (James 5:15 NIV)

I FIRST BECAME AWARE OF THE GIFT OF HEALING AND
God's power and willingness to heal while still a child.
My grandmother often suffered from migraines and
would ask me to put my hands on her head to ease
the pain. All I recall is asking Jesus to make her better,
placing my hands on her forehead and scalp, and feeling
a warmth flowing between us. I didn't know this was
healing prayer—it was just something I did in response
to my grandmother's pain. Back then, the church had
very little to say about healing and the ministry to which
God calls so many of us, both lay and ordained.

In the healing ministry, we often see wonderful and
indeed miraculous results, but even when there is no
obvious answer to our prayer, I believe wholeheartedly
that no one ever asks for healing and is denied. We are
not always healed of the bodily or mental ills which
most concern us, but healing is given in accordance
with our deeper needs, known to God if not always to
us. Often it is in the most secret parts of mind and spirit

that healing first takes effect, as God refines us to fulfil his purpose and prepares us for his kingdom. This was certainly my own experience, both on a personal level and when ministering to others.

In the late 1980s and early 1990s, John and I were involved in the healing ministry at our parish church, serving alongside a team of people who had been trained and commissioned for this ministry. We saw many examples of God's healing power at work over that time. One of my favourites also taught me a very important lesson concerning trusting in God, discerning his word, and stepping out in faith.

At the end of a morning service, a young woman came to John and me for prayer. She was almost twelve weeks pregnant but was anxious about her baby because she was experiencing symptoms similar to those of a previous pregnancy when she had suffered a miscarriage. Her fear of also losing this baby was tangible. As we prayed and I laid hands on her, I was given a vision of the baby waving a hand at us. I didn't know what to do. What if this was my imagination and not a sign from God? How devastating would it be for this young woman's faith if she were to be reassured by this vision only to miscarry her precious babe?

I prayed silently for God to give me a sign as to the accuracy of what I'd seen. Nothing. Frantically, I continued my silent prayer. Ages seemed to pass, although it was actually only moments. Still nothing. I began to feel hot, almost boiling in my skin, and ready to explode. Suddenly the words tumbled from my lips, and I heard myself sharing the vision I'd seen. The young woman was overjoyed and immediately felt a deep sense of peace and confidence that all would be well. She was convinced that the scan which she was due to have the next day would show that the baby was thriving.

That proved to be the case, but she shared with us something else that I shall never forget. During the scan, the technician suddenly pointed to the screen and said, 'Look, it looks just as though your baby is waving to you.' What a confirmation! This was exactly what God had shown me as we ministered to her. Needless to say, the pregnancy continued without any problems, and in due course she gave birth to a beautiful healthy boy. God is indeed good.

When serving in the healing ministry, we are also faced with the difficult question of why everyone isn't healed when we pray in faith. It is a question to which none can give a satisfactory answer for those at the sharp end of suffering and need. Many far better equipped to answer than I have tried, but their answers have too often been confusing or even hurtful, leaving the sufferer feeling guilty rather than loved.

All I know is this: God is far wiser than we are and does not always answer our prayer immediately or on our terms, as I experienced myself. Thinking that we know what is needed, we need instead to ask the Holy Spirit to guide us in what we pray for. We don't necessarily know what is best. Sometimes there are other matters which our Heavenly Father is dealing with first, and sometimes the answer is simply, 'No, my dear child, I want to take you home.'

Whatever the reason for the apparent delay or lack of healing, we must not give up but must listen to what he is saying in the situation. God does answer prayer and is full of love and compassion for us, healing us first in those areas he knows to be essential in the broadest terms of our needs. I have several times encountered situations when those for whom we prayed received no cure for the sickness from which they suffered but did come into a deeper understanding of God's love for them and thus a right relationship with him before they died. If that is not healing at its most important level, then what is?

'Healer, heal yourself!' Ministering to others and witnessing God's miraculous power and presence, I nevertheless continued to decline as the MS gained a firmer foothold on my life. Yet I never gave up hope or lost faith in God's love and willingness to heal those who turned to him. Somehow, I knew I could trust in him. In Jeremiah 29:11, we read:

> "I know the plans I have for you," declares
> the Lord, "plans for welfare and not for
> evil, to give you a future and a hope."

Those words rang so true to my ears. Hadn't I experienced God's faithfulness and love since early childhood? Whatever the future held, I could trust in God to see me through.

In January 1992, my life changed forever. John and I went with our vicar and other members of our healing ministry team to a healing ministry training weekend led by the late Reverend Peter Hancock, then UK warden of the International Order of St Luke the Physician. OSL is an ecumenical order dedicated to encouraging and supporting the Christian healing ministry within our churches.

I had been struggling with an exacerbation of the MS and wasn't sure that I could physically cope with the weekend. I sensed that I had reached a crossroads, and the time was fast approaching when I would be unable to be as effective a teacher as my pupils deserved and as I wanted to be. A few days before, I had promised John that if matters had not drastically improved after the weekend, I would go to my doctor and ask him to begin the process of helping me to obtain early retirement on the grounds of ill health. It was a watershed moment, and my spirits were low. I felt as though I just wanted to sleep and not fight the effects of the exacerbation, but I also really wanted to attend the training course. We prayed for God's strength, and I said, 'Lord, if you want me there, you'll need to give me the strength', and he did.

As the weekend drew to a close, we were offered individual prayer for healing. By then, I wasn't sure that God *wanted* to heal me completely of MS, though I knew he could. So I asked for healing to enable me to continue teaching for a bit longer so that we could see our daughter through her training as a chiropractor, a costly business which needed my income in order to meet the expense. I'll never forget Peter's response. His eyes twinkling, he said, 'Oh, I think God can do better than that!' Then he laid his hands on me and prayed for complete healing from the disease. Apart from my feeling of utter peace and confidence that all would be well, nothing appeared to happen.

Later, we ministered in teams of three at the public healing service. As the ministry time was drawing to an end, I was standing with my two prayer partners, our hands joined as we prayed for some people who had been unable to attend the service. My vicar approached to say that he had received a word to pray with me. As he laid his hands gently on my shoulder and head, he prayed, 'Lord, please show Chris exactly how you want her to serve you.' The next thing I knew, that I was lying on the ground bathed in light. My first thought was, God's having a laugh.

For some time the charismatic movement had been growing in strength. We often had teams visiting the area, holding revival-style meetings and offering prayer for healing. On several occasions whilst receiving ministry, I had felt the person ministering to me putting pressure on my forehead, pushing me backwards and sometimes rocking me slightly. This infuriated me. I sensed that they were trying to induce me to collapse to the floor and 'rest in the Spirit', a sure sign in many people's opinions that God was at work. I wanted no part in such chicanery. Others spoke of similar experiences, and I made it clear that I would 'rest in the Spirit' at God's behest and not to massage someone's ego!

But on this occasion, as I lay on the ground I had no doubt who had put me there. I had been holding the hands of my ministry partners seconds before, standing firmly on my own two feet without any balance issues. Our vicar's hand on my head had been feather-light, no pushing or rocking there—I could almost hear God chuckle! As I lay there feeling utterly at peace, deep within my soul I heard God's voice, 'Chris, I am calling you to serve me as a priest. Will you obey my call?'

I was astounded. I had sensed God calling me to something for some time, and John and I had discussed whether God might be wanting us to serve in some new way now that our children were beginning to step out into their own lives. We had even bought a property in rural France with the thought of moving there once I took early retirement and running the smaller cottage as a gîte in the holiday season. We envisioned holding healing retreats out of season, charging the bare minimum to cover costs in order to make them more accessible.

The possibility of ordination had been suggested on more than one occasion by various people, and there had been moments when I sensed a pull in that direction but swiftly discounted it as my imagination. So sure was I that it was a nonsense that I had never even mentioned it to John, much less to our vicar. After all, the Anglican

Church was not considering ordaining women—indeed, the national synod had recently rejected such a possibility. Quite apart from that, I was certain that I was most definitely not a suitable candidate. Finally, no diocese would ever consider even starting the selection process with a person who had MS.

Despite all of this, as I lay there stunned by what I had clearly heard, I found myself responding, 'Yes, Lord, if that is your will, but it will have to be in your strength alone because I am woefully inadequate.'

Dazed and wondering, I shared with John what had happened. He was annoyingly unsurprised! It seems he had sensed for some time that I had this calling and was wondering when I would finally wake up to it. I can't say that I noticed any physical change in how I was feeling, any more than I had after Peter's ministry, but I knew that I could trust our Lord and went to sleep excited but at peace. Had I known the extent of the demands this new path would place upon me, would I have felt as peaceful? I don't know.

When I awoke the next morning, everything had changed. Our normal routine was for John to get up around 6.00 a.m. and bring me a drink and my medication, which helped ease the dizziness. I would wait for the tablets to take effect before getting up, as the mornings were the worst time for the dizziness and I would often fall if I got out of bed before the tablets had done their work.

This particular morning, shortly after John went to make a drink, I felt the urge to 'spend a penny'. Before I knew it, I had jumped out of bed and made my way to the bathroom. I was on my way back to the bedroom when I realised what had happened. No dizziness; no staggering or falling. Then I realised that the constant tingling and sense of exhaustion were gone. Tentatively, I checked myself over. Nothing! That is to say, I had none of the usual symptoms with which I had learned to live. It was as though God had given me a new body.

Even as my spirit soared with praise and thanksgiving, a part of me was urging caution lest it be a vain hope. 'Get thee behind me, Satan!' How the devil loves to pull us back from reaching out to the fullness in Christ that is offered to us through God's grace and love. Throughout that day, I found myself running checks on my body. This was real: God had healed me completely. Not one vestige of the symptoms remained, and I have never experienced them since.

You can imagine the joy in our hearts and the celebrations when we shared the news with our family, church family, and friends. Many, like my doctor, were bemused and spoke of a remission. But remissions don't heal the damage caused by the scarring or their effects, nor do they usually last for decades.

If I or anyone else needed any proof of the thoroughness of the healing that I had received, it was given that summer. We were in France, reroofing the main house.

John hates heights but can manage to cope if he can stay pretty much in one place. So he was sitting up on the roof, placing the clay pantiles while I ferried the fresh tiles up to him and stacked them nearby. I grew up climbing trees and the cliffs near our home and had absolutely no fear of heights. So climbing up and down the ladder held no problems for me.

Imagine the scene: it's a hot sunny day, and the roof is two stories up from the ground. Time and again, I climbed up the ladder one-handed with a stack of heavy clay tiles under the other arm. Before being healed, I could not have climbed a ladder even using both hands; my balance was way too precarious. Neither could I have carried the stacks of clay tiles—remember, prior to the healing, my arm wouldn't even hold itself up long enough to write a few words on the blackboard, much less make the tiring journeys to and fro as I ferried the tiles up to John at regular intervals throughout the day. What an amazing God we have!

With the healing of the MS began a long and often tough journey that would challenge my faith and commitment. The Synod still had not approved the ordination of women within the Anglican Church, and yet I knew without a shadow of doubt that this was my destiny. God had called me and healed me, and now I had to step out in faith and start the process that would eventually lead to my ordination. I had no idea when this would be. I only knew that as God was faithful, so must I be. Had I known what lay ahead, would I have had the courage to take that first step? I believe so, if only because I had experienced something utterly amazing, a true miracle, and I had a debt to pay.

Before going on to explore what happened next, I think it would be helpful to place my situation regarding ordination in context. So here is a quick overview regarding the ordination of women in the Anglican Church at the time—more 'glass ceilings'.

With all forms of discrimination, change occurs only when people of conviction take a stand and campaign tirelessly. The major organisation to campaign for women to become priests in the Church of England was the Movement for the Ordination of Women (MOW), which operated from 1979 to 1994.[1] The MOW General Synod Steering Committee usually met once during each session of the Church of England General Synod to discuss policy and strategy on measures affecting the ordination of women. Among these, the most relevant to this book included the Deacons (Ordination of Women) Measure, July 1983; Women Lawfully Ordained Abroad Measure, November 1983; and the Ordination of Priests

---

[1] Greater detail on the work of this vital movement can be found in Fabiana Barticioti's 'Archive of the Movement for the Ordination of Women' of 1 December 2016, which can be found in The Women's Library collection at LSE Library. Papers in the archive date from the early 1970s to the mid-1990s and cover the organisation's running, offering a close insight into its campaigning strategy and the struggles encountered by its campaigners. For further research go to Women at LSE, https://blogs.lse.ac.uk/lsehistory/2018/04/04/women-at-lse-1895-1932.

(Ordination of Women) Measure 1991. The Steering Committee advised the central council and the executive committee on matters arising and were the link among MOW, members of the General Synod, and the Houses of Laity and Bishops. Committee members included bishops, clergy, and lay ministers. It should be noted that at this point there were many men, both lay and ordained, who campaigned tirelessly alongside the women, and their contribution was invaluable.

The call for the ordination of women was far from new even in the early 1970s; indeed, the concept of women priests began to be discussed in the 1920s, and the first woman to become a priest in the Anglican Communion was Florence Lim Ti Oi in 1944, in Hong Kong in response to the crisis among Anglican Christians in China caused by the Japanese invasion. To avoid controversy, Reverend Florence resigned her licence, though not her priestly orders, at the end of the war.

However, it was not until thirty-one years later, in 1975, that the Church of England General Synod passed a motion stating it had 'no fundamental objections' to the ordination of women to the priesthood. Despite this positive affirmation, a motion to remove legal barriers to the ordination of women was defeated in the House of Clergy at the General Synod meeting on 8 November 1978.

Years of campaigning followed until the Priests (Ordination of Women) Measure finally was passed by the General Synod on 11 November 1992. The law was granted royal assent on 5 November 1993, as in order to pass the measure, it was necessary to obtain the consent of the Queen and Prince Charles. The ordination of the first women took place in a service at Bristol Cathedral on 12 March 1994, when thirty-two women were ordained as Church of England priests at a service officiated by Bishop Barry Rogerson. The women were ordained in alphabetical order, so Angela Berners-Wilson is considered the first Anglican woman to be ordained.

At the time, many churchgoers were far from happy with the ordination of women, and the Archbishop of Canterbury, Dr George Carey, who had backed the proposal, said he recognised the result would not please everyone. 'What binds us together in God's love as a Church', Dr Carey said to the General Synod, 'is vastly more important than a disagreement about women's ordination.'

However, his attempts to keep the Church united had a setback. Four hundred vicars were so opposed to the idea of women priests that they fled en masse to the Roman Catholic Church—with many returning to the Anglican Church within a year or two.

Those who opposed the measure continued to make their objections known, and some parishes were obdurate in their assertion that they did not want women as priests. So the Synod and House of Bishops had to find a solution that would protect the interests of those who would not accept women priests. It is worth noting that no provision was made to protect those women newly ordained from the nastiness of many who opposed their ordination.

As a result of pressure from the opposition, two resolutions were introduced. Parishes could hold an extraordinary general meeting at which these were discussed and voted upon. The decision had to be revisited at intervals in order to ensure that this was still the view of the parish or benefice, and the resolution could be rescinded at any time, provided two thirds of the church membership was present.

> **Resolution A.** That this parochial church council would not accept a woman as the minister who presides at or celebrates the Holy Communion or pronounces the Absolution in the parish.

> **Resolution B.** That this parochial church council would not accept a woman as the incumbent or priest-in-charge of the benefice or as a team vicar for the benefice.[2]

In order to satisfy detractors further, yet more measures had to be put in place, because some stated that they could not remain under the leadership of any bishop who chose to ordain women to the priesthood. As a result,

---

[2] Priests (Ordination of Women) Measure 1993, 5 November 1993, legislation.gov.uk/ukcm/1993/2/enacted.

the role of Provincial Episcopal Visitor (PEV), popularly known as a flying bishop, was created via the Episcopal Ministry Act of Synod 1993).[3] Under this act, provision was made that if the local bishop participated in the ordination of women as priests, a parish could request to be under the pastoral and sacramental care of another bishop who had not participated in such ordinations. In this event, the parish still remained in the diocese of the local diocesan bishop, but said bishop might invite the 'flying bishop' to make his visitation.

Note that whilst immense amounts of time and energy went into the creation of these measures to meet the requirements of those opposed to women priests, at no point in the Church of England's history were any measures put in place to meet the needs of those who had equally strong and theologically based reasons for wanting the ministry of women priests.

Contrast further the reactions of the two factions when the Synod's decisions were made: when the vote went against the ordination of women, there were scenes of great jubilation among those opposed which were shown on national television. Yet when the 1993 vote for the ordination of women was taken, those supporting it were told that should it be passed, it would be inappropriate to be celebratory—because of the pain such a decision would cause the opponents! We were asked, therefore, to

---

[3] Bishops and Priests (Consecration and Ordination of Women) Measure 2014, legislation.gov.uk.

avoid scenes of public celebration should the vote go in our favour, and we did. Still no level playing field, then!

One has to ask, did any in authority have any concept of the hurt and pain the first decision to reject the ordination of women had caused, or of how much women had suffered in the preceding years? Those scenes of jubilation by the opponents to the ordination of women were every bit as hurtful to us as any we might have indulged in following the passing of the measure would have been to its opponents. It was as though a woman's call to ordination could be swept away as a foolish dream, of no consequence. Yet over the years, a great many women have sensed and longed to respond to that call—and were denied the opportunity to explore it further. Equally, many men and women have felt very strongly that in refusing to ordain women, the church was failing to follow our Lord's teachings, and this was a great source of pain.

Since the ordination of women as priests began in 1994, dioceses generally have on the bishop's senior staff a Dean of Women's Ministry (or Bishop's Adviser in Women's Ministry, or similar), whose role it is to advocate for clergy who are women and to ensure that the bishop is appraised of issues peculiar to their ministry. These advisers convene in a national association, The National Association of Diocesan Advisors in Women's Ministry.

The ordination of women in the Anglican Communion has been increasingly common in certain provinces since the 1970s. Some provinces, however, and certain dioceses within otherwise ordaining provinces, continue to ordain only men, whilst other provinces ordain women to the three traditional holy orders of bishop, priest, and deacon. A few provinces ordain women as deacons and priests but not as bishops; others still ordain women as deacons only.

Here in the UK, it was to be many years before women were to be permitted to enter the episcopate. The process was as long drawn out, painful, and convoluted as its predecessor which had allowed the ordination of women to the priesthood. In 2005, 2006, and 2008, the General Synod of the Church of England voted in favour of removing the legal obstacles preventing women from becoming bishops. The process did not progress quickly because of problems in providing appropriate mechanisms for the 'protection' of those who cannot accept this development.

On 7 July 2008, the Synod held a debate lasting more than seven hours on the subject, narrowly voting in favour of a national statutory code of practice to make provision for opponents. More radical provisions such as separate structures or overseeing bishops, proposed by opponents of the measure, failed to win the majority required across each of the three houses (bishops, clergy, and laity).

A plan suggested by a revision committee, released in a statement in October 2009, was intended to vest some functions by law in male bishops who would provide oversight for those unable to receive the ministry of women as bishops or priests. This created widespread concern both within and outside the Church of England about the appropriateness of such legislation. In the light of the negative reaction to the proposal, the revision committee subsequently announced the abandonment of this recommendation. The wrangling continued for a further five years as proposals were rejected, refined, and rejected again in attempts to provide the concessions demanded by those opposed to women's ministry. Then, at its meeting on 7 February 2013, the House of Bishops decided that eight senior women clergy would be elected regionally to participate in all meetings of the house until such time as there were six women bishops sitting as of right.

In May 2013, the House of Bishops expressed its commitment 'to publishing new ways forward to enable women to become bishops'. In July 2013, the Synod decided to reintroduce legislation to be addressed in November. At this General Synod, a package of measures was approved as the next steps towards allowing women to become bishops.

Further debate in February 2014 resulted in draft legislation being sent to all the dioceses of the Church of England. All dioceses that were able to meet within the necessary time frame (43 of 44) approved the draft legislation in time for it be debated at the General Synod in York in July 2014. On 14 July 2014, that legislation passed all three houses of General Synod, achieving the two-thirds majority required in all three. It gained the necessary parliamentary approvals and royal assent in the subsequent months, to be finally approved by the General Synod on 17 November 2014.

The first woman to be ordained as a bishop in the Church of England was Libby Lane, whose appointment as Bishop of Stockport (a suffragan see in the Diocese of Chester) was announced on 17 December 2014. She was consecrated at York Minster on 26 January 2015. Next, on 25 March 2015, Alison White was appointed Suffragan Bishop of Hull, also in the Diocese of York and consecrated at York Minister on 3 July 2015.

The third woman to be appointed bishop, and the first to be a diocesan bishop, was Rachel Treweek, whose appointment as 43rd Bishop of Gloucester was announced on 26 March 2015. She became Bishop of Gloucester on 15 June 2015 following the confirmation of her election. On 22 July 2015, she and Sarah Mullally (Bishop of Crediton, a suffragan see in the Diocese of Exeter) were the first women to be ordained as bishops at Canterbury Cathedral.

Pursuant to the Lords Spiritual (Women) Act 2015, which makes time-limited provision for vacancies among the Lords Spiritual (the bishops who are members of the House of Lords) to be filled by diocesan bishops who are women, Bishop Treweek also become the first woman bishop to sit in the House of Lords, where she was introduced on 26 October 2015.

Those opposed called for special measures to meet their needs and for 'protection' from the ministry of female bishops. However, at no point was any form of alternative oversight or ministry offered to those of us who did not wish to receive them from either priests or bishops opposed to the ordination of women. Our only option was to move parish or diocese or both.

4

Ordination and Beyond

You have laid your hand upon me.
(Psalm 139:5b NIV)

MY FIRST STEP ON THE JOURNEY TO ORDINATION WAS TO talk with my vicar. I was still quite overcome by the healing I'd received, and his matter-of-fact acceptance really steadied me. 'I wondered how long it was going to be before you realised God was calling you to ordination', was his response. It echoed that of my husband, John, who has been my rock and constant support, not only through the selection process but throughout my ministry.

The response of others was varied, largely depending on the level of their faith and understanding that God does indeed still heal today. Our immediate family, along with our church family, were elated and full of thanksgiving to God, as was the Reverend Hancock from OSL, who had ministered to me at that fateful weekend. Christian friends were equally elated, especially those who had been sure I was called to ordination. For others, the best they could manage was a cautious acceptance that I was in an excellent 'remission'. (Said 'remission' has now lasted for almost thirty years!)

My next step on the journey was to have a meeting with our diocesan director of ordinands (DDO). If he was at all surprised by or sceptical at what I had to tell him, he certainly didn't show it. Within a very short time, he had set up appointments for me with three of the bishop's advisors. These three individuals were tasked with talking with me about different aspects of my call to ordination, my spiritual life, and family circumstances.

In due course, I was told that I would be sent to an ABM (Anglican Board of Ministries), basically a long weekend of closest scrutiny by three individuals with the wisdom and experience to discern the calling of potential ordinands. There was still no decision regarding the ordination of women, so my application could only be for ordination to the diaconate. The understanding was that once the ordination of women was approved, my status would automatically be changed to ordination to the priesthood.

Before being sent on a selection conference for the ordained ministry, I had to go to London to be examined by the Anglican Church's medical advisor. I love his response once his examinations were complete:

> This is possibly the scariest moment of my life. I am a Christian and I believe in God's power and willingness to heal today but I am also a doctor and have before me all the medical evidence to prove that you have had MS, which is an

incurable disease. Now, having examined
you, I have to write a report declaring
that you are 100% fit and free of MS.

The first available place on an ABM selection conference
was in early October, but some months beforehand I was
contacted by the diocese inviting me to begin training
at the South West Ministry Training Course, starting in
September. How could I possibly do that before being
selected? I was understandably confused. It seemed that
there was only one other woman starting on the course
that September, so they wanted us to support each other
through what would be a very male-dominated process.
Since this request was sanctioned by the bishop, I agreed,
albeit reluctantly.

So in September I began training. Part of this involved
travelling to the University of Exeter each week for two
years to study on the Diploma in Theology course, which
formed a significant part of our training. Exeter is about
a forty-five minute drive from our home town, and I
shared this weekly journey with two other ordinands,
Colin and Geoff, and Colin's wife, Kate. These three
became good friends and were later to provide huge
support and encouragement.

A few weeks after term began, I attended the ABM
selection weekend. Along with the others present at that
weekend, I had completed a long application form in
advance, which often formed the basis of the individual
interviews held over the weekend. In addition, we had

various 'tasks' to complete. One of these left me outraged! We were required to write a pastoral letter, the scenario being that we were writing to an old friend who had been the best man at our wedding. The way in which this was couched made it obvious that this was aimed at men, and no allowance had been made whatsoever for the fact that there were several women applicants on this weekend!

I struck out that designation and replaced it with 'chief bridesmaid'. Maybe that's why they turned me down! Yes, that's what happened. Shortly after my return I was contacted by the DDO to give me the news. The assessors had not been able to reach a unanimous decision in my favour, so could not recommend me to the bishop for ordination. Apparently, despite having the right to ignore the advice of the assessors, our bishop had never chosen to do so. So that was that.

In the debrief, I was told that the main concern had been that I would 'frighten the pants off male clergy colleagues'. What an insult to the excellent male colleagues with whom I have been privileged to serve over the last twenty-two years. However, on reflection, I can understand the concerns. Had I been selected, I would have been among the first women to be ordained, having been selected to train as a priest. (Those women who were already deacons and felt called to the priesthood were ordained very soon after the decision in favour of the ordination of women.)

The decision to ordain women to the priesthood was made later that month, and at the time of the ABM there was a high level of confidence that the Synod would agree to this. There were many people who for a variety of reasons opposed this measure, and the introduction of women priests was going to be fraught with difficulty and dissension. Little wonder then that the selectors were erring on the side of caution.

I was a woman of independent mind, well accustomed to holding my own among male colleagues, and I was also a team leader. Strong-willed, unafraid of authority, and admittedly something of a control freak, I was probably very far from the quiet, unassuming, and compliant type of woman they needed just then!

The decision caused a great deal of controversy and upset in the diocese, and our vicar wrote a furious letter of complaint. It was, in his view, a clear case of discrimination. The points that were highlighted as giving cause for concern about my suitability had also been highlighted at his selection, but in his case were seen as positive indicators. More glass ceilings!

I was utterly shattered and simply could not understand what had happened. God had called me and healed me, and yet the door was firmly shut in my face. How was I to comprehend this? My own hurt and confusion was compounded by that of my family and many friends and supporters. I was told that selectors are only human and sometimes make mistakes, and I was encouraged to continue with the diploma and reapply in two years' time. (It was mandatory at the time to wait two years before reapplying for selection.)

I didn't know what to do. Prayer for guidance gave no clear-cut answers. I was in turmoil. I am so grateful to the many people who encouraged me to stick with it and trust to God's timing. Significant among these were my three travelling companions, Kate, Colin, and Geoff, who encouraged me and supported me on our weekly trips to Exeter. During the two years' wait, they as much as my husband and family gave me the strength to face another selection conference.

I remember very little from this conference, apart from one instance. Early on, I was chatting with other would-be ordinands who were questioning me about my former conference, trying to get an insight into what they might expect. Mindful of the instruction not to go into details about this, I tried to be encouraging but vague. Imagine my outrage upon discovering that one of the selectors who passed by at that moment later accused me of 'holding court'.

I left that conference determined to accept whatever decision was made and not to consider applying again if I were turned down. Oh the pain, the hurt, and the confusion! Yes, it happened again: they turned me down. Apparently, I had caused total confusion and sharp disagreement among the selectors with the result that the obligatory unanimity was not reached.

However, God was not finished with me yet. I was summoned to see the bishop, who informed me that he was 'not mindful to accept the recommendation of the selectors' and that he wished me to commence training for ordination to the priesthood the following September. I could not believe my ears. This went completely against his previous record in this regard. Despite this, I was still unsure and informed him that I would only commence training if the principle of the South West Ministry Training Course (SWMTC) was given a copy of the assessors' findings and having read it was willing to accept me on the course. What a cheek, giving ultimatums to one's bishop! Would I never learn?

Less than twenty-four hours later, I received a call from David, the principle of SWMTC. He made it very clear from the outset that he believed that the assessors had got it completely wrong and that I should listen to those within the diocese who knew me and accept the invitation to begin my training for ordination. His conviction gave me the courage to say yes, and so in September 1996 I began training for ordination to the priesthood. Ordination followed in 1999, and I was priested the following year. God works in wondrous and often unimaginable ways. To him be glory and praise forever.

When I began my curacy, the ordination of women was still a new thing within the Anglican Church, and for many it was an extremely painful time. I know of women priests who, when wearing their 'dog collar', were spat on in the street. Others struggled with unkind remarks and ostracism from male colleagues. I was very blessed and had wonderful support from my male colleagues and the majority of the congregations I served.

For the most part, those whom I encountered who opposed the ordination of women were gracious and showed true Christian principles. For many in opposition, the move to ordain women cut deeply, and many left the Anglican Church. Others, however, realised very quickly that women were excellent priests, bringing a new dimension to the ministry, and I know personally of a number who admitted that their opposition had at its root pure gender discrimination.

One such opponent was a parishioner, Michael, who lived in one of the parishes where I served my curacy. He had served that parish faithfully for many years and had been in the forefront of those encouraging the parish to pass measures A and B. During my diaconal year, I was asked by their vicar, who wholeheartedly supported the ordination of women, to set up a monthly family service at that church, and I also served as a deacon at some of the main services.

Michael and I got on very well, despite our differences, and when he became very ill, the vicar asked me to take him Communion each week. As the elements had been consecrated by the vicar, Michael had no problem with receiving it from me. Then, shortly before my ordination to the priesthood, several parishioners began saying how much they were looking forward to my ordination and asking when I would officiate at a Eucharist in their church. I explained that under the regulations surrounding measures A and B, I would not be permitted to celebrate the Eucharist in the church.

This caused some consternation, and I was amused and somewhat gratified to be told that those rules didn't apply to me, and that they wanted me to perform my priestly role there as well as in the other churches in our team. Once they realised that we had to stick to the rules, a special general meeting of the parish was called, and measures A and B were thrown out with just one abstention and none against.

Just a few days prior to the meeting, Michael showed me a letter that he had written to be read out at the meeting as he was too ill to attend in person. In it he stated his belief that his previous opposition to the ordination of women had been based on prejudice and that his experience of my ministry had shown him very clearly that I would be an excellent priest. He offered his vote in favour of removing the measure and asked others to do the same. I was amazed and quite overcome, both by Michael's humility and his acceptance of my calling.

There was more to come. Michael offered me a small, ancient box and asked me to accept it. He told me that it contained a travelling Communion set that had belonged to his great grandfather. Michael explained that there was no one in the family who would be particularly interested in this heirloom and said, 'I can think of no better hands in which to place it than yours.' I was moved to tears and have never forgotten those words. The little porcelain Communion set has been a precious reminder of the way that God can change long-held prejudices, and I still use it occasionally when taking Holy Communion to the sick.

It can still be rather a rather rocky road for ordained women; even today, many find that they are not operating on a level playing field. Slowly, however, things are changing. Even so, not only does underlying legal discrimination still exist but vehement opposition is still in evidence, from campaign groups such as Forward in Faith and Reform (the former a predominantly Catholic grouping opposed to women's ordination, established as an umbrella organisation after the 1992 vote, and the latter an evangelical group created in 1993 who also campaign against women's ordination).

As previously noted, parishes can instigate legislation to stop women priests working in their church, so there are still very clear pockets of opposition creating what Dyer[1] (1999) has called 'no-go' areas. For a woman, finding a post in such areas would prove impossible.

In total contrast to the extended discussions and planning that went into providing for the needs of those opposed

---

[1] 'Revisioning the Reception - five years of women priests' published in 'ANVIL' the Journal of Theology and Mission vol 16 No. 2 1999. Church Mission Society.

to the ordination of women, suitable maternity provision for female priests was not pre-empted in any way. Indeed, those who had been the first priests to need maternity leave recalled how church officials often resorted to asking the women themselves what the provision should be. In some cases, dioceses had nothing in place and had to think quickly in order to put organisational systems in place.

Research indicates that 'there is an underlying thread that if women cannot give birth, hand in assignments, fulfil college duties and attend worship then they are not as reliable and dedicated as male candidates, putting a black mark against their gender'[2] Moore, 2008. Thankfully, appropriate legislation is now in place, and matters are much improved.

---

[2] 'Women in Ministry – Equally Called' Beth Moore Fuller Seminary 2008.

5

We Pray; God Heals

> Almighty God, who inspired your
> Servant St Luke the Physician to set out in
> the Gospel the love and Healing Power of
> Your Son. Make obvious in your Church
> the same power and love to the healing
> of our bodies and souls through your Son
> Jesus Christ our Lord. Amen. (Prayer of
> the International Order of St Luke the
> Physician)

FOLLOWING THE HEALING THAT I RECEIVED AT THE
training weekend led by the Revd Peter Hancock, then
UK warden of OSL, John and I researched the order and
decided to join. The OSL is a Christian healing order
dedicated to promoting the Christian healing ministry,
offering training and support for churches and assisting
them in setting up healing ministry teams. The order
sees the healing ministry as complementary to rather
than as a replacement for medicine, and we pray regularly
for our local hospitals, health centres, and their staff.

Members of the OSL are encouraged to live by a simple
rule of life, namely:

- I will pray daily for this work, remembering to use the Lord's Prayer with the special intention that God's will may be done in me and in all humankind. I will also use the special prayer of St. Luke's day at frequent intervals.
- I will cultivate a personal prayer life, and will seek to become closer to Jesus Christ, our Saviour and Healer.
- I will pray for the whole body of Christ for the purpose of supporting the scriptural intent that the whole body "build itself up in love."
- I will read from the New Testament daily.
- I will receive Holy Communion regularly.
- I will seek such health of body, mind, and spirit as will make me capable of maximum vocation.
- I will cultivate the gifts God has given me for the work of healing by study and active service.
- I will seek continued growth as an instrument our Lord can use for the healing of others.
- I will share this Healing Gospel with others by personal witness, by praying with others, by supporting Healing Ways, the Order's journal of healing, by circulating healing literature, and by contributing according to my ability.
- I will attempt all of this so far as I am able with the help of God.[1]

---

[1] Manual for Members of the International Order of St Luke the Physician (amended Apr 2011). Further information on the International Order of St Luke the Physician may be found at www.orderofstluke.org.uk.

When the OSL was originally formed, the Christian healing ministry within churches was almost non-existent, and many people had fallen into the error of believing that the age of miracles had passed. Even St Augustine, in his early ministry, fell prey to this error, for in his early writings he claimed that healing had ceased within the church and was no longer a necessary part of its mission. After becoming a bishop, however, he found out about more than seventy miracles that had taken place over just two years. Subsequent first-hand experience led him to reverse his original stance. In 427, just three years before he died, Augustine wrote *Retractions*, in which he took back what he had said in previous writings. He went on to describe the miraculous cures that he had witnessed and that had caused him to change his mind.

Fortunately, most Christians now realise that the age of miracles is still very much present among us, and there are few churches that do not have a healing ministry. Indeed, within the Anglican Church, it was the focus of a report on the healing ministry for the House of Bishops entitled 'A Time to Heal: A Contribution towards the Ministry of Healing'. The report laid out clear guidelines for dioceses and parishes in terms of developing good practice within the healing ministry:

> Each parish should evaluate ways in which the healing ministry is carried out as part of mission, and make proposals for improved effectiveness, noting local

needs, challenges, and expressions of this
ministry in ecumenical partnerships.[2]

Recommendations of the report also included the provision of appropriate training for ordinands and the provision of advisors for the healing ministry within dioceses.

Nowadays, there are many resources available, from books to courses to training weekends and conferences, which encourage and equip this vital ministry. My husband I have written and further developed a training manual for the OSL here in the UK that is offered free to any churches wishing to use it.

For both John and me, the healing ministry has been, and still is, a central part of our lives and work for the Lord. We have been privileged to witness his hand at work and have seen many people healed. Over the years I have spoken at many conferences and training weekends, both nationally and internationally, putting my teacher's training as well as my theological training to good use and encouraging people to be a part of this ministry which is so central to the Christian faith.

Contrary to what some people imagine, the healing ministry is not the province of a privileged few who have received a special gifting of the Holy Spirit. Far

---

[2] A Time to Heal: A Contribution towards the Ministry of Healing, Chapter 14 (Church House Publishing: The Archbishops' Council, 2000).

from it, and indeed such a view is unscriptural. The Gospel of Mark makes it very clear that Jesus extended the ministry of healing to all who believed in him:

> And these signs will accompany those who believe ... they will place their hands on sick people and they will get well. (Mark 16:17a 18b NIV)

John also gives us Jesus's words on this matter: "I tell you the truth, anyone who has faith in me will do what I have been doing" (John 14:12 NIV).

When we trust in the Lord and step out in faith, amazing things happen, for we do not minister in our own strength but in his. He is the healer, not us, and to him goes the glory. The key is to stay close to him through prayer and reading the Bible and to listen carefully to him. Often, our Lord speaks in unexpected ways: through scripture, the words of others, images or visions, and that still, small voice within.

Have you ever felt prompted to speak to someone or to do something and sensed that it is the Lord's prompting? Have you then ignored the prompting because acting upon it might be embarrassing or because you are not certain that it is of God? A good test of the latter is to ask yourself whether it is something that Jesus would do or approve of. If the answer is yes, then follow it through and watch what our amazing God does.

The more you respond to our Lord's promptings, the

more confident you will become, and the more you will see his hand at work. Over the years, John and I have experienced this in many, often very different ways. Our awesome, loving God never ceases to amaze us. A few years ago, John and I were en route to New Zealand, where I was due to speak at a conference. We arrived at King's Cross station feeling hungry and thirsty. We had plenty of time before we needed to set off for the airport so decided to have a meal at one of the cafes on the station.

Unfortunately for us, there were no empty tables at our chosen café, but the Lord prompted us to ask if we might share the table of a fellow traveller. As we hesitated, a lady called us over and indicated that there was plenty of room at her table and that she would soon be leaving anyway. We thanked her and sat down, and she chatted about her journey as we waited to place our order.

Then I felt the Lord prompting me to tell her that we were off to a healing conference, and this opened the gates for her to share her need of healing prayer. Her daughter had recently lost a baby and in her grief was struggling to cope and face life. We prayed for her, her husband, and our table companion, asking God's healing and grace. Our companion left for her train a few minutes later, telling us that she was sure God had sent us to her and that she believed he was healing her daughter. We never saw her again, but we do believe that God answered her prayer.

Sometimes, when God sets up one of his 'divine appointments', as we call these encounters, we are not so ready to follow his call: it's inconvenient, we're tired, we have other matters on our mind. However, we know from long experience that these promptings are not something we can ignore. We are here to serve him, and we delight, mostly, in doing so.

I said 'mostly', and one such reluctant response occurred on our journey home from our dream holiday. I had just retired, and we were fulfilling a long-held ambition to do some serious travelling, something that we'd had little opportunity for in the past. Thanks to an inheritance from my mother's sister, Ruth, we were able to fulfil our dream.

Our last stop on the three-month-long 'round the world' trip was in Savannah, where we were to spend some time with my cousin, Eden, and her husband. Our flight arrived in Atlanta in good time, but we discovered that the onward flight to Savannah, booked many months previously, was no longer scheduled. The next available flight was not for another two hours. We knew that Eden and Furman would already be on their way to meet us, so we were very concerned at the delay.

Fortunately for us, God was ahead of us, and a few moments after receiving this news, we were told that there were two spare seats on the flight that was about to depart. It was going to be a rush to get to the departure gate on time, and we were further advised that our luggage might not make it to the plane, in which case it would have to go on the next flight. As it turned out, we and our luggage made it.

We were fortunate in being seated together, and as we settled in, the lady in the next seat greeted me pleasantly. We exchanged a few words before I reached for my book. I was tired and a bit stressed from the journey so didn't really want to chat to a stranger at that moment. However, God had other ideas—it was no coincidence that we were unexpectedly on that flight and sitting with this lady. Another 'divine appointment' had been arranged!

The familiar prompting was met by a degree of reluctance on my part, but with an inward sigh, I laid my book aside and turned to my neighbour. Taking more notice of her now, I could see that she was distressed, and after a little gentle prompting, she shared the cause. She had been to visit her much-loved mother-in-law. They had a close and loving relationship, but this visit had been very difficult. Her mother-in-law was suffering from dementia and had been very angry and unpleasant at times, which was totally unlike her. 'I don't know how I'm going to tell my husband about the deterioration in her condition or what the best thing for her is going to be long term," she confided.

I found myself telling her that I was an Anglican priest and offering to pray for her. I have made such an offer on many occasions in the past but couldn't remember any previous occasion when I felt prompted to mention that I was a priest. However, as usual, God had a purpose. The lady reached out to me with an expression of joy on her face. 'You're the angel I was praying for. I felt so distraught that I asked God to send me a minister of the church to pray with me. And here you are.'

John and I prayed with her for God's peace and guidance for her and her husband and for healing and peace for her mother-in-law. Before going our separate ways, I gave her my card. The next day, I received an email from her husband, thanking us for our prayers and telling us what a difference they had made. I felt humbled and also a little ashamed—it would have been so easy to shrug God's promptings aside and miss that important divine appointment.

These unexpected appointments can sometimes involve us in a degree of inconvenience, as when our hire car's battery failed on a journey in unfamiliar territory, where the terrain meant we also had no signal for our phones. We had pulled off the main road to drive down a track in order to eat our picnic lunch beside the river. Unlike our own car, this one did not turn its headlights off automatically when the engine was switched off nor give any warning that the lights were still on!

And so as we prepared to resume our journey, we found that the battery would not turn the engine over. Now what were we to do? Offering up a prayer for divine assistance, we decided to try and 'bump start' the car. As we were struggling to do so, a couple cycled into view with their dog. Seeing our plight, they stopped to help. It turned out that their home was only a few minutes' ride away, so they offered to fetch their car and some jump leads to start our engine.

On their return, we chatted as the men set about the business in hand. Our rescuer told us that he was a farmer but had struggled to manage his farm over the past year as the result of a back injury. We offered to pray for him, which he accepted with alacrity. He too was a Christian and so recognised God's hand on this encounter. We gave thanks for the healing God gave him.

These divine appointments aren't always about physical healing. Sometimes God has other matters on his agenda, as on the occasion when we got chatting with a taxi driver. He told us that he was a believer but rarely attended church. He had two small boys and really wanted them to grow up knowing God. We were able to direct him to a church that would suit his family and prayed with him for God's outworking in their lives as a family.

As in that situation, God gives us that small point of contact and a job to do for him, even if our contact with those to whom God is reaching out is brief and transient. We are like small cogs in a far greater wheel, but what we are called to do or say at that brief moment in time can have enormous effect.

One of my least favourite occasions for God to nudge me into action is when he suddenly awakens me in the early hours of the morning. I am a deep sleeper and have been known to slumber blissfully on through thunderstorms and earthquakes, but that divine nudge has me wide awake in seconds. All vestiges of sleep are gone, and I am clear-headed and alive to his promptings.

The first time this happened, I had no idea why I was suddenly and rudely awakened … until I sensed God's words: 'Pray for Michelle. She needs your prayers now.' It was a little after 2.00 a.m. Startled, but certain that this was a divine command, I woke John.

How blessed I am to be married to such a prayer warrior! Unperturbed at this sudden awakening, he sat up to pray with me for Michelle, a childhood friend who lived some eight hours' drive away from us. We were not given any clear idea as to why this was necessary, but we knew our prayers at that moment were vital. Having prayed, we had a strong sense of peace and were fast asleep in no time.

The next morning I phoned Michelle's husband, Ray, and he had an amazing tale to tell. Michelle had been rushed into hospital and undergone emergency bowel surgery. Her condition was so critical that she was close to death, and he was desperately anxious. They were nominal Christians but had no church connexions, so sending out a call for prayer was not something familiar to him. It was around 2.00 a.m. that he had an urge to phone us and ask for prayer, but didn't like to disturb us at such an hour. God had no such compunctions!

At the time that we were praying, Michelle's life hung in the balance. Then, quite suddenly, she had taken a turn for the better, and the crisis was over. But what was the purpose of this miracle? God certainly doesn't need our help, so why involve us? I believe with certainty that our involvement was meant as a witness to our friends and as an unforgettable lesson to us to respond unquestioningly to our Lord's call.

Another such occasion was much closer to home, when we were about to become grandparents for the second time. We were very excited. Our son, Pierren, and his wife, Katie, were expecting their second child. Sadly, their first had been miscarried early on in the pregnancy. This time, however, everything had gone smoothly, and both Katie and the baby were doing well.

It was 27 January 2011 when we received a phone call from our son that Katie was in labour and they were at the hospital. At this time, they were living in Den Hague in the Netherlands. We waited anxiously for news. Katie was an older first-time mother, and we prayed that all would be well for both her and the baby. The labour was protracted, and we spoke with our son again just before going to bed at around 11 p.m. We prayed again for Katie and the baby and for the medical staff at the hospital before finally falling asleep.

Suddenly, I was wide awake with that familiar sense of our Lord's presence and the urgent need to pray for Katie and the baby. I looked at our bedside clock, it was just after 4.30 am. Surely she wasn't still in labour? Poor Katie. I woke John, and with a mounting sense of anxiety we began to pray. It's one thing to pray for complete strangers but quite another when it is for beloved members of one's own family, even when one has absolute confidence in God's loving compassion and power.

A tight knot formed in my stomach as I pleaded with God to protect mother and baby and to guide the medics caring for them. A feeling of peace and certainty that all would be well washed over me as the words 'I am Yahweh Rophe, the God who heals' filled my mind. We looked at each other. Echoing my unspoken thoughts, John said, 'It's going to be all right. We can go back to sleep now.' Despite all the tension and anxiety that we had felt initially, we fell sound asleep.

Next morning, we phoned our son as early as we dared and were overwhelmed with gratitude to our mighty, loving God as Pierren shared the events of his daughter's birth. As we knew, it had been a long, drawn-out process. The baby's shoulder had jammed in the birth canal, and she wasn't moving; mother and baby were exhausted. Suddenly, the room filled with medical staff and equipment, and Katie was surrounded by frantic activity.

The baby was finally brought into the world, but the cord was tight around her neck and she was blue. In moments, the skilled team had her freed from the cord and in an incubator, whisking her off to the intensive care unit, where she remained for the first few days of her life. When we saw her a couple of days after her birth, she still had tubes attached to her tiny arms.

Jessica was born at 6.02 a.m. on 28 January 2011, her grandpa's sixty-fourth birthday. When we compared times, allowing for the time difference between the two countries, we realised that we were awakened to pray just as things reached crisis point.

Under the circumstances, there was a very real concern that lack of oxygen might have caused irreparable damage, but praise God, this was not the case. Indeed, a few years later, Jessica was tested by an educational psychologist because her teacher was convinced, as were we, that she came within the gifted and able spectrum. Following confirmation of her high IQ, she was offered a place in the Mind Plus Academy, which she attends one day a week, spending the remaining four days in her local primary school. Recently, at age ten, she was selected by Otago University to take part in their national maths challenge.

We were all very grateful for the care and expertise of the medical staff at the hospital where Jessica was born, but John and I also continued to thank God for his protection of this precious granddaughter. We shared with Pierren and Katie our experiences at the time of Jessica's birth but felt they were inclined to give credit to the hospital medical team rather than to God.

However, God was not finished with them, and confirmation of God's healing and protection came a couple of years later.

By then the family had moved to Aberdeen, and Katie had become friends with another mother, who was also a midwife. Comparing notes one day, Katie shared what had happened at Jessica's birth. Her friend was astounded and said it was nothing short of a miracle that Jess had come through undamaged. We were filled with joy when Katie told us about the conversation and prayed that this would help Katie and Pierren to grow in faith.

Not all of God's promptings concern healing. One such call occurred just a few months ago. As I write, Covid-19 still grips our nation, and we are very well aware of its devastating effects on the lives of many. Our church runs a food bank on an estate where many are suffering deprivation. John and I help with the foodbank and in October sensed God calling us to include fruit and vegetables along with the store cupboard items already provided. Fruit and vegetables are expensive, and we are well aware of their importance for the immune system so knew how vital it was for people to have them in their diet. As usual, God had matters in hand. We spoke with our church's Community Pioneer on the estate, only to find that she had received the same message and was wondering how to put it in place.

Our church family already gave generously to the food bank; could we ask them to do more at such a difficult time for so many? We sensed that we should put our faith in God and start providing the fruit and veg. We worked out that we could manage about £50 per week in the short term and £25 in the long term. With the help of a local supplier who provided the fruit and veg at cost, we managed to buy enough for the families needing this extra provision at an average of £45 per week.

However, God's provision was already there, as another member of our team contributed a further £10 per week. Then, at a Zoom virtual coffee morning held by our Soroptimist club here in Sheffield, I mentioned the new venture. Several members later messaged me with the offer of funds. Within ten days I had received donations of over £200.

Even total strangers donated to the cause. One day, overhearing me chatting to our supplier, another customer handed me a twenty-pound note towards the fruit and vegetables. On another occasion, a young man from the estate dropped in at the food bank and gave us £20. More recently, a charity, hearing of our work, donated £500. In addition, other members of our congregation have made regular donations specifically for the fruit and veg.

Sadly, as the effects of Covid have bitten deeper into our nation's economy, our food bank has found an ever-increasing number of people in need of help. As I write, numbers attending weekly have more than doubled since October 2020, and our weekly fruit and vegetable bill is now around £85. Thanks to the generosity of many and our Lord's provision, we are able to meet the increasing demand and provide a greater supply to those in need. God is indeed faithful when ordinary people heed his call and step out in trust.

6

All Are Called

There is neither Jew nor Greek, slave nor
free, male nor female, for you are all one
in Christ. (Galatians 3:28)

THE ABOVE TEXT REMINDS US THAT ALL ARE EQUAL BEFORE
God. No one is better than another or more important or
valued; we are all equally precious to him. Throughout
his ministry, Jesus demonstrated this in many ways,
especially through his treatment of women, lepers,
sinners, and outcasts as well as those who thought they
had a right to people's respect and obedience.

God values our contributions to his kingdom equally
too. Whatever we do to help another, however small
that might seem, is valued by him, and recognised as
being for him as much as for the actual recipient: 'Truly
I tell you, whatever you did for one of the least of these
brothers and sisters of mine, you did for me' (Matthew
25:40 NIV).

A smile, a kind word, small practical deeds to help in
some way, a listening ear or encouraging word—all can
make a huge difference to another. The greater our love

for God, the more we want to serve him and the more ready we are to serve others in whatever way we can. It's not done for personal gain or to 'buy' our way into heaven. Our ticket to heaven is already paid for by our Lord's blood on the cross, and all we have to do is open our hearts and lives to him.

Always remember: following our calling as Christians to serve as Christ taught us to is not centred upon doing great things for God but rather on offering ourselves as vehicles through whom our all-powerful God will perform his mighty works.

Don't let anyone, especially your own view of yourself, convince you that you are unworthy or ill equipped to serve God. That is the lie of the devil. God will use the least of us in amazing ways, and when he calls us to serve him, he also equips us. His Holy Spirit, our guide, comforter, and enabler, is given to all who acknowledge Jesus as Lord and Saviour. What we do for the Lord, we do in his strength; our own inadequacies and past failures don't get in the way.

If you find this hard to believe, then read the Bible and look at those Jesus chose to do great works for him. Uneducated fishermen became his first disciples; many with obvious character flaws were builders of his church. One who denied him to save his own skin became the leader of the early church and was given unthought-of authority and spiritual gifts. Another who at first was set on exterminating this new Christian faith became one of its greatest teachers and leaders, founding churches all over the Middle East and Europe.

Look back over the history of the Christian church and you will see again and again how God has called the weak, the disenfranchised, the outcast, the sinful, and diehard opponents to serve him—and then worked through them to build up his kingdom here on earth. His redeeming work through Christ can transform each of us beyond our wildest dreams.

I have been privileged to call as friend one whose early life with its dysfunctional upbringing and perceived inadequacies would appear, by human standards, to bar her from doing great things in God's service. For her, there was an industrial strength glass ceiling firmly fixed just above her head; or so it seemed.

Yet God shattered that completely and called her into his service. Her obedience to his calling and trust in the equipping of his Holy Spirit has transformed not only her own life but those of countless others. What follows is her story, which I am privileged to be permitted to share with you now.

Her name is The Revd Sister Jane Emson and she was born into a dysfunctional family where she suffered neglect and abuse from her earliest years. Constant verbal abuse and a total lack of affection were all she knew. The family lived a very hand to mouth existence on a tough estate in Sheffield. Jane would often run away to her dad and grandmother but was always brought back.

She had four older brothers and, at an early age, became the general 'skivvie', even though she was the youngest. She was expected to cope with all of the cleaning, washing and ironing. Punishment for not completing everything was to be barred from going out with her friends. This was the worst thing for Jane as she was surrounded by lots of friends and loved to be with them. So Jane would sneak out to join them when her mum was out and get a hiding when her mum caught her.

Jane was often kept off school to do housework etc and this, combined with the undiagnosed dyslexia from which she suffered, resulted in her making very little academic progress. She suffered the stigma and hurt of being called 'thick' and other equally damaging names.

As soon as she was old enough to do so, Jane got a paper-round but all the money earned from her paper-round and later from baby-sitting, had to be handed to her mother. Jane didn't really mind about the money as working got her out of the house.

As a result of her experiences, Jane had no sense of self-worth and no aspirations; inevitably, she was soon drawn into a destructive lifestyle. She left home at sixteen and went to stay with a brother and his wife; but when her brother was sent to prison she had to move on. Jane 'sofa-surfed' for some time and ended up in difficult and often abusive relationships, living life 'on the edge'.

She still craved love and attention from her mum, running

to her at her beck and call and always remembering her on her birthday and at Christmas, but the abuse continued. The longed-for loving mother-daughter relationship seemed a lost hope.

Unsurprisingly, Jane became pregnant, but the baby, Michael, who was very premature, died at the age of a year and two weeks. Jane's mother had never acknowledged Michael and the father was not around so all through the time that Michael was in and out of hospital Jane had to cope alone. It was a very dark period for her, with no real support and she soon found herself in a very volatile relationship. Unable to sleep without sleeping tablets, Jane got a job at a sweet factory working nights, hoping that this would help her to cope.

A while later, Jane met another young man, and they began a relationship. Things were really good for a time, and she became pregnant with her daughter, Rianna. While Rianna was still a baby, she and Jane were taken to a mother and baby refuge. Jane really wanted the relationship with her partner to work and to have a stable family life, so she returned to him and tried again. The births of her two sons, Jimmy and Johnny, followed. Unfortunately, her dream of a happy family life wasn't to be.

Meanwhile, Jane's mother was having a difficult time with two of her sons and Jane tried to support her. Sadly these two brothers have since died of alcohol and drug abuse.

When Jane came to faith in 1995 and she and the three children were all baptised, she started to pray for her mother and their relationship began to change. Her mum became very different in her attitude towards Jane and her children and would often visit them. She even apologised for the way she had treated Jane in the past. Their relationship became what Jane had always hoped for and her mum began to ask about God.

Sadly, while in hospital on what they thought was a routine visit, she died with Jane sitting beside her and holding her hand. Tragically, this is the only memory Jane has of ever holding her mother's hand. For Jane, there was a real sense of God's presence there in that hospital room and she is convinced that her mother sensed it too. Several times before she died, her Mum asked Jane to turn off the light in the room as it was too bright to need it. Was she seeing God's glory surrounding her? Jane believes that this was so.

One consequence of Jane coming to faith was the courage it gave her to make the final break with her partner. Helped by her church family, she found the strength to start afresh. Even so, left to bring up her three young children alone, all of whom were under the age of seven, Jane knew hardship and suffering but this only increased her generosity of heart. She has been helping disadvantaged families and evangelising ever since.

Looking back at all that Jane had endured and the chaotic lifestyle this brought, her life might well never have changed were it not for two things. Firstly, God awoke in her heart a desire to know him and then led her to a church where she met a lady whose one desire was to serve him.

This lady's name is Sister Sandra (Church Army) and she reached out to Jane and her children with love, compassion, and acceptance. This is the second reason for the change in Jane's life and illustrates how small acts of kindness and acceptance can set in train an entire series of events that will change lives in unimaginable and unlooked for ways.

These are Sr Sandra's words, written for an article published in the OSL (UK) magazine, 'Healing Ways', which I edit, and included here with her permission and blessing.

"Do angels go on walk abouts today? Perhaps the following will help you decide. One Sunday morning a young single mum called Jane and her three young children walked into the church where I worked as a church army officer. My main area of work was with children/families and youth. This was during an interregnum.

Someone who Jane had never met before invited her along to church. I had never seen the person before either and as I am always on the look- out for new people coming through the door to welcome them in, I am sure I would have known if she had been before.

Jane never saw that person again. We both now think that person was an angel.

We invited Jane and family for Sunday lunch, my husband Roy said, "The joint I put in the oven before we came out is too big for just the two of us and I can soon do a few more veg." Jane and her children came to church just about every Sunday after that. So they weren't put off by our food!"

After a few weeks, Sandra asked Jane if she would help in Kidzone, she was a bit shocked and nervously rubbing her hands together said something on the lines of, "Well, you will need to show me what to do."

Sandra spent time with Jane on a one-to-one basis, sharing the Gospel and helping her to understand her role in Kidzone. She saw the potential in Jane and recognised her love for God, so some time later she invited Jane to help her with school assemblies.

Later, after praying about it, Sandra suggested to Jane that she train as an evangelist in the Church Army. Her response was that she felt God calling her to train at Cliff College in Derbyshire.

As Sandra expressed it, "God knows what He is doing, while there, Jane was diagnosed as dyslexic and got the help she needed; two years later she came out of the college with an Honours degree in Mission and Evangelism! I might just add that she was working at the same time alongside some very needy young families."

In time, Jane did apply to train as a Church Army Evangelist and during that period she sensed God calling her to be ordained. By then, she and I had met and got to know one another through our church. Jane was our pioneer evangelist, working on a very deprived estate in our parish.

Many of the people there had experienced the same levels of deprivation, rejection and suffering as Jane herself and they recognised one of their own. Jane chose to move onto the estate, in order to be among the people, and her passion for God and for sharing the Gospel were like a candle flame burning bright in a dark place. She was often referred to as the 'Pied Piper' as the children would follow her and seek her out. Her home became an oasis for many of them.

As well as bringing many to Christ, Jane also introduced a number of initiatives to help improve the lives of the people among whom she served. Whilst supported in her work by members of our congregation, my husband and myself included, central to all of her work was the recognition that the people of the estate should take ownership of what was happening there and so she trained volunteers with the intention of enabling them to run the various projects themselves.

Through all of this, Jane changed so many lives for the better, making known to them God's love for each of them as individuals and building up their faith as well as striving to help them to improve their quality of life.

I became her Spiritual Director and encouraged her to listen to God and test her calling. It was indeed a testing time for Jane, she did not fit the perceived picture of an ordinand any more than Jesus' first disciples fit the perceived image of leaders within the Jewish faith. Discouraged and doubting her calling, Jane shelved her quest for ordination and focused on God's call to a new ministry on two very needy estates in Middlesbrough. However, God's hand was still firmly upon her and her calling.

She moved to Middlesbrough in July 2019 and just fourteen months later I had the privilege of attending her ordination as a Distinctive Deacon in York Minster on Sunday 27th September 2020, along with Sr Sandra. She has since been invited to explore ordination to the priesthood.

It was no easy thing for Jane to follow God's call to Middlesbrough. She was leaving behind in Sheffield her family, friends and all with which she was familiar. We continued to talk and pray together regularly and I encouraged her to seek out another Spiritual Director nearer to her new home. I remained her mentor and we, along with many others, especially Sr Sandra, continued to pray for her and her new ministry.

Jane is a shining example of what God can do in the lives of those who choose to follow him. When we place our trust in him and look to the Holy Spirit's equipping, there is no barrier or glass ceiling big enough or thick enough to hold us back from serving him, in what might appear to be seemingly impossible ways. Recently, Jane was nominated to receive a Community Award for her work.

To a group of young people who came from deprived and dysfunctional backgrounds, Desmond Tutu once said, 'What you need to realise more than anything else, is that your PAST doesn't have to define your FUTURE. You are a VSP—a very special person. You're made in the image of God and you have the potential to change the world. God doesn't create rubbish, each of us is special to God and YOUR name is engraved on HIS hand! The most important thing you can do is to remind people they are special to God.' (emphasis mine).

If this little book does nothing else, I pray that it will encourage you to fulfil your God-given potential, as Jane has done, and to step out in faith to become all that God has created you to be. Remember, you are precious to God and nothing can change his love for you. With God, all things are possible, and glass ceilings are soon shattered.

About The Author

The Reverend Christine Low is an Anglican priest, now retired from full-time ministry, and a former UK National Director of The International Order of St Luke the Physician. In addition to training ministry teams, Chris has been a guest speaker and seminar leader at many healing conferences both in the UK and abroad.

She is married to John, a retired teacher, and they have two adult children and two granddaughters. They divide their time between their home in Yorkshire and the North Island in New Zealand.